# STRENG'
# NATURAL IMMUNITY

*A Plant-Based Macrobiotic Approach*

## EDWARD ESKO
## ALEX JACK
## BETTINA ZUMDICK

**Foreword by Martha C. Cottrell, M.D.**

Berkshire Holistic Associates
PLANT BASED NUTRITION & LIFESTYLE

Published by Berkshire Holistic Associates
A Division of Planetary Health, Inc.
A 501(c)(3) Educational Organization
305 Brooker Hill Road
Becket, Mass. 01223
BerkshireHolistic.com

Published in Association with the International Macrobiotic Institute and the Culinary Medicine School

InternationalMacrobioticInstitute.com
CulinaryMedicineSchool.com

Second Edition June 2020
ISBN: 9798630014931 (paperback)

Front Cover: Ume plums after spring rain

### Note to the Reader
The guidelines and suggestions presented in this book are for educational purposes. They are not a substitute for qualified medical attention. Those who suspect serious illness in themselves or family members are advised to seek prompt medical attention. If, on the other hand, you need guidance in adopting a plant-based diet and lifestyle, feel free to consult a qualified macrobiotic counselor.

The coronavirus (COVID-19) is a respiratory illness that can spread from person to person. The Centers for Disease Control and Prevention states that the virus that causes COVID-19 spreads mainly between people who are in close contact with one another. The virus can be contracted from respiratory droplets produced when an infected person coughs or sneezes or by touching a surface that has the virus on it and then touching their face.

PHYSICIANS COMMITTEE FOR RESPONSIBLE MEDICINE

# Contents

# FOREWORD

I am a healthy 92-year-old woman, a physician who discovered the role our diet plays in promoting health or disease. I was never taught this in medical school. Also, I was never taught to look for the cause, but rather to treat symptoms. Now, here we are caught up in the "threat" of the coronavirus, and once again, looking for a "treatment" rather than addressing the fact, as reported in the *New York Times*, that 88% of Americans are sick and on some kind of medication!

In all the information that has come to the public, this fact has not been presented. These people are very vulnerable to viruses, any virus, and are the most apt to die. Just look around and be amazed, shocked at the number of people, including children and young people, who are obese. Look at what people are loading up their grocery carts with and you will see the cause of their poor health and vulnerability. You'll see lots of meat and dairy. Soft drinks. "Junk" food! And what does this have to do with their vulnerability, or to illness in general? *It's the immune system, stupid*! Let me share with you a simple lesson in understanding the immune system.

When we eat the meat of mammals, drink their milk, and eat milk products, our immune system recognizes this as a "foreign body" and builds an antibody against it. As this circulates through the body, it attacks our own body, becoming confused, because we too are mammals, but "different." The Chinese taught thousands of years ago, "Eat as far from your own species as possible." So wise…and as we are developing increasing knowledge of the immune system, we are amazed at their knowledge so long ago.

When I discovered this over forty years ago, I had many medical problems and was on a number of prescription drugs. I changed my diet, got off of meat and dairy, and began to practice a plant-based diet with occasional fish, nuts, and lots of veggies, organic whole grains, sea veggies, and miso soup. I used acupuncture for my arthritis. I had severe rheumatoid arthritis and arthritic psoriasis. I also suffered from asthma, sinusitis, and gallbladder problems. Within 6-8 weeks all the symptoms went away. I was amazed!

I changed my practice from treating symptoms to searching for a more comprehensive approach such as diet, work, and family—stress of lifestyle. I saw remarkable results, including the reversal of certain illnesses, including cancer, heart disease, arthritis, and others. I have been teaching this approach for almost fifty years and here I am 92 years old—on no medications, healthy of mind, body, and spirit and still enthusiastically sharing with all who want to change their diet and lifestyle and promote their health, developing a strong immune system and living free of "symptomology"—changing the "cause."

Martha C. Cottrell, M.D.
May 2020

# PREFACE

———

*On the first day of spring, Thursday March 19, 2020, macrobiotic friends, counselors, students, practitioners and chefs attended an online class given by Edward Esko, macrobiotic teacher and founder of the International Macrobiotic Institute, to discuss the macrobiotic approach to understanding and dealing with the emerging Coronavirus pandemic.*

*Most of us in the northern hemisphere were looking forward to the Spring Equinox as we had put away our snow shovels and heavy winter apparel in anticipation of early spring flowers and warmer days. But this year we usher in spring's warmth along with fear and anxiety. COVID-19, a novel coronavirus that results in respiratory distress and for many, failure, had begun spreading rapidly throughout the United States.*

*Social distancing is now the norm as the virus changes how we function individually and as a society. As schools, colleges and universities close their doors, learning continues, online. The following is from our special coronavirus online session, held on the Spring Equinox. —Paula Pini*

The outer coating of bacteria, the outer skin, is made up of carbohydrate and fat. Viruses have a hard spikey shell made up of protein. Inside is a cavity filled with genetic material known as RNA. A bacterium, on the other hand, has a soft outer coat but is dense and solid inside. Thus, viruses are yang at the surface and yin on the inside, while bacteria are yin at the surface and yang at the center. Antibiotics, which are yin, thus act on bacteria by neutralizing their yang inner core. However, antibiotics have no effect on the yin central core of the virus.

The novel coronavirus is covered with spikes known as glycoprotein-s. You've all seen the images. COVID-19 resembles a World War II ocean mine. These devices were designed to sink ships. Like the virus, mines are spheres with spikes protruding from their surfaces. What happens if a ship touches one of these spikes? The mine explodes and tears a hole in the hull, often resulting in the sinking of the ship. The shell of the mine is made of yang metal, just like the shell of the virus. Inside the mine is nitrogen explosive, highly yin, similar to the RNA at the center of the virus.

If the s-protein spikes come into contact with receptors on the surface of a human cell, something like an explosion happens, similar to an exploding mine. The virus bursts through the cell's protective membrane and releases RNA into the interior of the cell. Viral RNA fuses with the cell's DNA (RNA is yin; DNA is yang), forcing the cell to begin replicating viruses. The cell will eventually explode and release the next generation viruses into the bloodstream. This process repeats over and over, resulting in a viral infection.

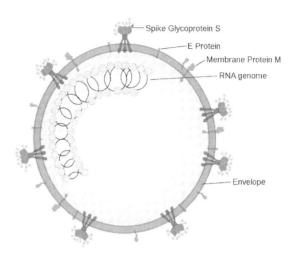

The coronavirus envelope is yang; the inside
is hollow, mostly empty, and yin

Viruses come in both yin and yang varieties, as do bacteria. With bacteria, we find gram-negative and gram-positive varieties. With viruses, some are mild, others severe. Some affect the upper respiratory passages; others affect the lower respiratory tract. Where, then, on the yin-yang spectrum of viruses is COVID-19? What are the factors that can help us determine whether the virus is yin or yang?

The novel coronavirus is carried through the air and inhaled. The respiratory system is at the frontline of the body's response to the virus. Like everything else, the respiratory system is divided into two: an upper and lower section. The upper respiratory tract is yin. It includes the nasal passages and throat, as well as the trachea and bronchi. The lungs are positioned lower and deeper, and are thus yang. The tiny air sacs, or alveoli, are the most yang or compacted.

Bronchitis affects the bronchial tubes, which are part of the upper respiratory tract. It is therefore yin. Pneumonia affects the inner regions of the lung, including the air sacs deep inside. It is comparatively yang. The symptoms of bronchitis are milder, while the symptoms of pneumonia can be severe. The symptoms of pneumonia may include a high-fever that can be life threatening.

Colds and flu are another example. Viruses cause both, yet one is yin and the other yang. Most colds last about a week, with their main symptoms being a runny nose, sneezing, sore throat, and a light cough. Colds affect the upper respiratory tract and are generally mild. The flu, on the other hand, is more severe. It includes fever and a dry cough. The virus that causes COVID-19 is generally mild, often producing no symptoms, but in certain individuals, it can cause serious complications. It has the potential to go deep within the lungs and cause respiratory failure. It can also attack the heart. These symptoms are strongly yang.

The novel coronavirus is zoonotic, meaning that it originates in animals and jumps to humans. The animals that are suspected—bats, civet cats (a type of raccoon), and pangolins (a spiny anteater) share certain peculiarities. All are carnivores. Bats eat insects, civet cats eat small mammals, and pangolins consume ants. Their diets are strongly yang. At the same time however, these creatures are nocturnal. The combination of a carnivorous diet and nocturnal lifestyle may provide the ideal breeding ground for viruses.

Sunlight, a more yang factor, weakens and kills yin viruses. Sunlight also strengthens the immune response. Bats, who live mostly in darkness, enjoy no such benefits. Lack of sun promotes the growth of viruses, while also weakening the immune response of the animal.

Most likely, over time, bats developed immunity to the viruses that developed within their bodies. Humans however, may or may not be able to resist these viruses. It is worth noting that all three of these creatures are eaten in China, and that may help explain COVID-19's jump from animal to human. Although the virus is transmitted through the air, it is also transferred through the digestive tract. A surprising number of cases in Wuhan, where the virus is believed to have originated, first presented with digestive symptoms, the main one being diarrhea.

Not only is diet a possible route for the transfer of novel viruses from animal to human, it is also a crucial factor in our ability to resist infection. Those with healthy immune systems generally show mild or no symptoms. In a small minority of cases, however, symptoms can be severe, life threatening, and fatal. Indications are that individuals in the latter group suffer a variety of pre-existing conditions such as type 2 diabetes, heart disease, obesity, and cancer, all of which compromise the immune system.

In a healthy individual, the immune system reacts to foreign proteins, such as those of virus and bacteria, by neutralizing and facilitating their discharge from the body. The immune response is sensitive, reactive, and highly efficient. It is also highly specific and adaptable, changing to meet the changing needs of the individual. It is not fixed or static, but dynamic and active. It is also strengthened or weakened by what the individual does on a daily basis, for example, by diet, activity, and exposure to immune boosting sunlight, or exposure to immune reducing stressors such as glyphosate, 5G radiation, and environmental toxins.

Between 70-80% of the body's immune cells are located in the digestive tract. How these cells function is largely determined by the health or sickness of the 100 trillion bacteria, known as the microbiome, that inhabit the digestive tract. The health of this internal ecosystem is determined by diet. These bacteria work closely with the intestinal immune cells, and vice versa. So called beneficial bacteria aid the immune response, while harmful bacteria weaken or confuse it. Writing in the journal *Cell*, March 27, 2014, researchers Yasmine Belkaid and Timothy Hand state:

> The microbiota plays a fundamental role on the induction, training and function of the host immune system. In return, the immune system has largely evolved as a means to maintain the symbiotic relationship of the host with these highly diverse and evolving microbes. When operating optimally this immune system–microbiota alliance allows the induction of protective responses to pathogens and the maintenance of regulatory pathways involved in the maintenance of tolerance to innocuous antigens.

Yin extremes such as antibiotics, sugar, food additives, glyphosate, drugs, and medications weaken the microbiome and the immune response. These extremes lead to a yin condition of immune deficiency. Persons who are obese, diabetic, or who are on medication are at greater risk for this condition. On the other hand, animal protein, parts of which are not fully digested, putrefies in the colon and increases the number of pathogenic bacteria. Partially digested fragments of animal protein also enter the bloodstream. Each of these effects triggers nonstop immune responses (yang), resulting in chronic inflammation. Individuals in either condition—inadequate or underactive immunity (yin) or hyperactive immunity (yang)—are at risk for the serious complications of COVID-19.

**Yin**—Underactive    Normal    Overactive—**Yang**
*Immune Deficiency*                    *Autoimmune Disorder*

Underactive immunity allows the virus to operate unopposed, and to penetrate deeply into the body's organs, infect cells, and overwhelm the organ's ability to function. Overactive immunity produces what is called a "cytokine storm," in which immune cells attack and destroy vital organs such as the lungs or heart.

How can we avoid these extremes and develop healthy natural immunity? The answer is simple. The whole grains, beans, vegetables, sea vegetables, seeds, nuts, and seasonal fruits in a macrobiotic diet strengthen the microbiome and the immune response. A plant-rich diet includes a great deal of prebiotic fiber, which serves as nourishment for beneficial bacteria. At the same time, a plant-based macrobiotic diet includes plenty of probiotic-rich foods that support and augment beneficial bacteria in the colon. These include naturally fermented miso, sauerkraut, natto, pickles, amasake, and others.

The answer to COVID-19 and other viral infections will not be found in vaccines. Rigid or one-size-fits-all efforts are doomed to end in failure. They do not recognize the dynamic and infinitely mutable nature of life, including the nature of the viruses and bacteria that are a product of the natural environment. The answer lies in strengthening our natural immunity through a healthful plant-based diet, together with adequate sunshine, exercise, and a balanced natural lifestyle.

Edward Esko
Paula Pini

# INTRODUCTION

Viral infections have the potential to spread around the globe. The *Washington Post* reports that 80 percent or more of the cases of the novel coronavirus are mild, even though many people have died.

In this time of heightened awareness and fear, it is most helpful to stay calm: you are likely aware that feeling fearful and stressed is creating elevated cortisol levels in the body, which suppress the immune function and derails many healthy bodily functions and thus make us vulnerable to the virus and other diseases.

On the other hand feeling joyful, having fun is boosting every defense and healing mechanism in our body.

Also, exposure to sunlight, regular exercise (especially outside in nature) and a healthy diet are boosting all systems in the body, as well accelerating any healing processes that may be needed.

We carry within us virus and other potentially detrimental pathogens all the time. Communication flashes between virus, microbes and body cells and they can change in the wink of an eye. Ideas and feelings of the most optimistic nature are ultimately our best protection.

As divine beings manifested in physical bodies we have all the power of creation: we get what we focus on.

When we focus on fear for any prolonged time we will create exactly what we fear the most.

Focusing on love and fun and joy for a large part of the day regularly will result in much more pleasant experiences. So: let's spend time feeling joy and love and raise our vibration!

Modern health research as well as ancient healing traditions suggest that eating a healthy diet, taking time to relax and enjoy, exercise, spending time outside, avoiding constipation, engaging in meditation and/or prayer support the immune system to fight off viral and other types of infection. Along with simple hygiene these measures are the number one way we can all protect ourselves and prevent the spread of disease.

Bettina Zumdick
March 2020

The gut is the seat of all feeling. Polluting the gut not only cripples your immune system, but also destroys your sense of empathy, the ability to identify with other humans.
Suzy Kassem

All disease begins in the gut.
Hippocrates

# Definitions*

---

## Yin

*The primary expansive force of the universe producing upward movement, lightness, an outside position, water and air, the colors green, blue, and purple, and the world of plants.*

## Yang

*The primary contractive force of the universe producing downward movement, heaviness, an inside position, solid matter, the colors yellow, brown, and red, and the world of animals.*

*Note: The terms "yin" and "yang" are Chinese in origin. Any terms that describe complementary/opposites may be used in their place.

# STRENGTHENING NATURAL IMMUNITY

*Edward Esko*

Virus and bacteria are part of the natural environment. They have been on Earth for several billions of years. Humans have coexisted with viruses and bacteria from the beginning; in fact, we couldn't exist without the colonies of beneficial bacteria that inhabit our digestive tract. When humans are living, and especially eating, with respect for the natural order, there is no need to fear viruses, bacteria, or any other part of the natural environment.

To understand what viruses are, and why they have such potentially negative effects, and also how to avoid these effects, let us consider the differences between viruses and the other class of infectious agent, bacteria. These differences are a perfect illustration of the complementary/opposites, known in macrobiotic and oriental medicine, as yin and yang. Yin represents primary expansive force; yang the primary force of contraction. The two forces animate all aspects of our environment. Therefore plants are more expansive and yin; animals are more contracted and yang. The cell nucleus is yang, while the cell membrane is yin. Plants that grow in a cold northern climate are more contracted, and thus yang; while those growing the tropics are more expansive or yin. In the Far North, there is little vegetation (yang.) The tropical rainforest is lush and expansive (yin.) Although both are carbon, a diamond is yang; graphite is yin. Gallstones and kidney stones are yang; hepatitis and fatty liver are yin. Pneumonia, which affects the deeper, more compact regions of the lung, is yang; while bronchitis, which affects the hollow and expanded bronchial tubes, is yin.

Clearly virus and bacteria have opposite characteristics. Bacteria are more biologically developed than viruses. They are single-celled organisms, while viruses are non-living. Bacteria tend to produce localized infection, while virus infections are often systemic. And, perhaps most importantly, bacteria respond to antibiotics, while viruses do not. Antibiotics, originally the product of rapidly growing mold, are strongly yin. They are used in the food industry to control infection, and also to promote the rapid growth of livestock. In nature, opposites attract and react. Similar things do not interact nor do they react. Thus bacteria, which attract and are subsequently neutralized by antibiotics, are yang. Viruses, which are not affected by antibiotics, are therefore yin.

Many viruses, including the novel coronavirus, bear a striking resemblance to World War II ocean mines. Both inflict damage if engaged. If left alone, they remain harmless. The outer shell of the ocean mine is made of metal, which is yang. The inner core is packed with nitrogen-based explosives, which are highly volatile or yin. Virus particles contain the viral genome packaged in a protein coat called the capsid. Like ocean mines, the explosive or yin portion, the genetic material, is located at the center, and the solid outer protein coat (capsid), is located at the surface. Thus, viruses are yang at the surface and yin in the interior. Bacteria are the opposite. Their outer coat, or capsule, is made up of more yin polysaccharide. Delicate, hair-like projections extend from the surface, in contrast to the thick spikes extending from the outer coat of a virus. The inner portion of the bacteria is comprised of a thick cell wall, cytoplasm, and chromosomes, all of which are more densely packed, or yang.

The spikes that protrude from the outer coat of the virus easily bond with yin receptors on the outer membrane of body cells. Once inside, the genetic material of the virus overwhelms the native genetic material of the cell. Rather than serve the needs of the cell, the alien genetic material causes the cell to begin reproducing new viruses. This yin, or expansive process continues until the cell explodes, releasing new viruses that go on to infect other cells, in a continually expanding process.

As we have seen, we divide infectious agents into opposite types: viruses and bacteria. However, each of these types divides into opposite subtypes. In the case of bacteria, there are gram-negative and gram-positive varieties. Among viruses, some are milder, others more severe; some last several days, while others persist; some affect the upper respiratory passages, while others move downward and attach to cells in the lungs. The cold and flu viruses offer a perfect example of these opposite tendencies. The differences between the cold and flu viruses are apparent: colds are milder; the flu is more severe. The flu lasts longer, while a cold goes away more rapidly. Colds affect the upper respiratory tract; the flu goes deeper, producing a dry cough. A cold is inconvenient; the flu can be fatal for those with compromised immunity. So, as we see, colds are yin; the flu is yang. Together with the behavior of a virus, the origin of the virus also offers a clue as to its yin or yang nature.

The animals associated with coronavirus infections share a number of characteristics. Bats are suspected transmitters of both SARS and COVID-19. Bats come in two varieties; more yang insect eating bats and more yin fruit eating bats. Civet cats, raccoon-like creatures, are also suspect. They are also carnivores. The pangolin, a form of spiny anteater, consumes ants and termites. Pangolins are also suspected in transmitting coronaviruses to humans. All three consume a yang diet—insects and animals—and are nocturnal. They are also eaten as food in China. This combination—a carnivorous diet plus nocturnal activity—may prove to be a breeding ground for a variety of coronaviruses, especially those that penetrate deep within the lungs yet spread easily from human to human. It may also help explain why viral outbreaks tend to be more severe in the cold and dark weather characteristic of autumn, winter, and nighttime.

The body has a number of immune responses to viruses. In a healthy individual, the immune system prevents viruses from infecting cells and causing damage. Viruses are neutralized by specialized cells of the immune system, including cytotoxic T cells and natural killer cells (NK cells) that destroy infected cells, and through the production of antibodies. In one process, yang antibodies cause virus particles to stick together, making them easier targets for immune cells than single particles. In another process, known as phagocytosis, phagocyte cells are activated by antibodies, triggering a process by which the phagocyte cell engulfs and destroys the virus.

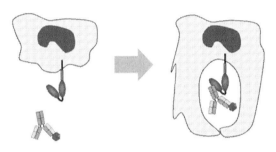

**Antibody mediated
triggering of phagocytosis**

The antibody actives the phagocyte cell
(top) to engulf the virus (bottom)

As we can see, the health of the immune system is vital in protecting the body from potentially harmful viruses. Much of the body's immune response occurs within the digestive tract. According to some estimates, the gut wall is home to 70 to 80 percent of the cells that comprise the immune system. Together with breaking down food and absorbing and producing nutrients, the digestive tract plays a vital role in the body's immune response. According to Andrew M. Platt of the University of Glasgow:

The large intestine (colon) has a large resident population of microbes, consisting of at least $10^{12}$ organisms per gram of luminal contents. These organisms, together with the antigenic load provided by the diet and the constant threat of potential pathogens, means the intestinal immune system encounters more antigen than any other part of the body.

The fact that a large proportion of coronavirus infections begin with digestive symptoms suggests that the intestinal immune system plays an important role in the development of the disease. In a study published in March 2020 in the *American Journal of Gastroenterology*, Chinese researchers examined data from 204 patients in Hubei province, believed to be the geographical center of the 2019 outbreak. Of these patients, 99 (48.5 percent) went to the hospital with one or more digestive symptoms as their major complaint. Symptoms included diarrhea, vomiting, and abdominal pain. According to the researchers, "Of these 99 patients, 92 developed respiratory symptoms along with digestive symptoms, and 7 presented with only digestive symptoms in the absence of respiratory symptoms. Among the 105 patients without digestive symptoms, 85 presented only with respiratory symptoms, and 20 neither had respiratory nor digestive symptoms as their chief complaint." Digestive issues were not only a first sign of illness, but also those who reported them tended to become sicker than those who did not. "Moreover, as the severity of the disease increased, digestive symptoms became more pronounced. Patients without digestive symptoms were more likely to be cured and discharged at the time of this study than patients with digestive symptoms." The researchers noted that 60 percent of patients with no digestive symptoms recovered, compared to 34 percent of those suffering from digestive symptoms. They further stated that, "Clinicians must bear in mind that digestive symptoms, such as diarrhea, may be a presenting feature of COVID-19 that arise before respiratory symptoms, and on rare occasions are the only presenting symptom of COVID-19."

Researchers at the Renmin Hospital of Wuhan University and the Wuhan Institute of Virology of the Chinese Academy of Science reported in February 2020 that the coronavirus might be transmitted through the digestive tract. They found genetic material of the virus in stool samples from patients, leading them to propose that the novel coronavirus may be spread through the fecal-oral route, as well as through droplets inhaled by the respiratory system.

This is one among many findings linking the condition of the lower digestive tract, especially the large intestine, with the lung and respiratory system. This relationship is mediated by the microbiome, the vast colonies of bacteria, most of which are beneficial, that inhabit the digestive tract. An article by Helen Fields published by Johns Hopkins in March 2020, entitled, "The Gut: Where Bacteria and Immune System Meet," states that a "huge proportion of your immune system is actually in your G.I. tract."

Although gut bacteria influence the body's overall immune response, their relationship to the lung is especially relevant to respiratory infections. The connection between the large intestine and lung is referred to as the "gut-lung" axis. In a paper by researchers Anh Thu Dang and Benjamin J. Marsland, appearing in the journal *Mucosal Immunology* in April 2019, the gut-lung axis is explained as follows:

The microbiota plays an essential role in the education, development, and function of the immune system, both locally and systemically. Emerging experimental and epidemiological evidence highlights a crucial cross-talk between the intestinal microbiota and the lungs, termed the 'gut-lung axis.' Changes in the constituents of the gut microbiome, through diet, disease or medical interventions (such as antibiotics) is linked with altered immune responses and homeostasis in the airways.

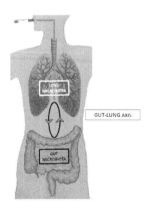

An understanding of the relationship between the lungs and large intestine is found in traditional oriental medicine, going back thousands of years

Further reinforcing this connection, researchers at the Francis Crick Institute discovered that disruptions in the intestinal microbiome resulting from antibiotics leave the lungs vulnerable to flu viruses and lead to more severe infections. As reported in *Science Daily*, in studies on mice, investigators found that signals from intestinal bacteria help to maintain a first line of defense in the lining of the lung. Eighty percent of mice with a healthy intestinal microbiome survived flu infection, while only a third given antibiotics prior to infection survived.

"We found that antibiotics can wipe out early flu resistance, adding further evidence that they should not be taken or prescribed lightly," explains Dr. Andreas Wack, who led the research at the Francis Crick Institute. Inappropriate use not only promotes antibiotic resistance and kills helpful gut bacteria, but may also leave us more vulnerable to viruses. "We were surprised to discover that the cells lining the lung, rather than immune cells, were responsible for early flu resistance induced by antibiotics," says Andreas. "Previous studies have focused on immune cells, but we found that the lining cells are more important for the crucial early stages of infection. They are the only place that the virus can multiply, so they are the key battleground in the fight against flu. Gut bacteria send a signal that keeps the cells lining the lung prepared, preventing the virus from multiplying so quickly."

A Google search on "diet, microbiome, and immunity" yielded many results. Research has shown that gut bacteria help develop immune cells, and also that immune cells help beneficial bacteria overcome the negative effects of harmful bacteria. High-fiber diets have been found to prevent microbes from eating away the lining of the colon, thus protecting against infection. Other studies have found that high animal food diets increase the risk of inflammatory bowel disease (IBD), while plant-based diets reduce risk and increase healthy diversity in the gut microbiota. Short chain fatty acids (SCFAs) are believed to improve colon health and lower the risk of inflammation. Researchers have found higher levels of SCFAs in subjects eating a plant-based diet, including a healthy Mediterranean diet. Plant-based diets high in fiber reduce intestinal transit time, or the time needed for food to travel through the digestive system. Protein breakdown was found to increase so-called "degradation" products in the colon. One of the researchers summarized the findings: "You can help food pass through the colon by eating a diet rich in fiber and drinking plenty of water. It may also be worth trying to limit for example meat, which slows down the transit time and provides the gut bacteria with lots of protein to digest." –*Science Daily*, June 27, 2016

Antibiotics and meat, the extremes of yin and yang, characterize the modern world. Both damage digestive health, the composition and function of the gut microbiome, and the body's immune response. Reliance on both extremes makes individuals more prone to serious infection by contagious viruses. The digestive system itself offers the necessary clues as to what to eat and what to avoid in order to maintain optimal digestive, microbiome, and immune health. It offers clues as to the optimal diet to build natural resistance to viruses and harmful bacteria. We see that a certain order becomes apparent both at the beginning of the digestive tract, in the mouth, and at the end of the digestive tract, in the colon.

An astonishing 100 trillion bacteria inhabit the large intestine. Here the ratio of "good" to "bad" bacteria is approximately 85% to 15%, or roughly seven to one. So-called "good" bacteria, such as lactobacillus and lactobacillus bifidus, are strengthened and augmented by the intake of prebiotics and probiotics. Prebiotics are undigested plant fibers and resistant starches. These serve as food for the bacteria in the digestive tract. Probiotics are the living organisms in fermented foods like miso, natto, amasake, and sauerkraut. These foods augment and strengthen the "good" bacteria in the colon. On the other hand, animal proteins decompose into a variety of harmful substances, including gram-negative bacteria, toxic metabolites, and ammonia.

A high-meat diet overwhelms the body's ability to digest the high volume of protein, so that as much as 12 grams of protein go undigested and unabsorbed, and enter the colon. Here the protein begins to decompose and produce harmful bacteria and other toxic substances. These bad actors are responsible for a variety of pathological, and potentially life threatening conditions, originating with a decline in natural immunity. The composition of the digestive microbiome suggests an evolutionary advantage to a diet based on grains and other plant foods.

The structure of the teeth supports the conclusion that plants should comprise the majority of the human diet. Of the twenty-eight plant processing teeth, the majority (20) are molars and premolars suited for crushing and grinding whole grains, beans, seeds, and other tough plant fibers. The minority (8) are the front incisors, which are well suited for cutting vegetables. Here we see that the ratio of harder, dryer foods such as whole grains and beans to softer and more watery vegetables is 20 to 8, or about 2 to 1.

Maintaining a 2 to 1 ratio of grains to vegetables conveys a number of advantages. Emphasis on the solid proteins in whole grains and beans helps ensure that one's diet provides a sustainable source of both carbohydrate and protein. Diets that de-emphasize whole grains and beans in favor of raw fruits and vegetables are often deficient in complex carbohydrates and protein. Furthermore, emphasizing grains and beans necessitates cooking. These plant fibers are hard and tough in their raw state and require softening to make them edible. Cooking (as well as soaking, sprouting, and fermenting) softens the tough plant fibers and facilitates smooth digestion, thorough absorption, and the efficient release of energy. Cooking is a form of pre-digestion that makes additional energy available to the body. It is also part of our heritage. Humans have been cooking food for at least two million years.

The nitrogen in protein increases the growth of bacteria, especially the harmful varieties in the digestive tract.

Eating less animal food, thus less protein, reduces the growth of harmful bacteria. On the other hand, carbon, such as that in plants, limits such bacterial overgrowth. Studies show that plant eaters have the highest levels of carbon and lowest levels of nitrogen in the colon. Meat eaters have higher levels of nitrogen and lower levels of carbon. According to Katrine Whiteson, a microbiome researcher at the University of California, "Generally eating lots of plants and getting a lot of fiber is likely to be a healthy diet, and that by nature would mean eating less nitrogen."

The implications for the current pandemic are readily apparent, in terms of the origin of the virus, its mode of transmission, and the susceptibility of individuals to either serious, mild, or no infection. All indications point to the protective value of a plant-based diet, and the necessity of ending our dependence upon animals as a source of food. First, the mishandling of wild and exotic animals is suspected as the origin of the virus and its jump from animals to humans. Secondly, the risk of infection increases with the level of immune dysfunction. Risk goes up as immune function goes down, in direct proportion. Stronger immunity equals less risk of infection. The evidence implicating a high meat diet in disruption of the gut biome, and thus the body's immune function, is clear. A diet dependent upon animal foods weakens natural immunity while providing a breeding ground for virus infection. Let us hope the current pandemic shakes humanity loose from its current dependence on animal food and toward a healthy and sustainable plant-based future.

# DIETARY PROTECTION FROM CORONAVIRUS

*Alex Jack and Bettina Zumdick*

As the world mobilizes to contain the coronavirus pandemic, a fundamental dimension of the crisis remains largely unrecognized: diet and environment. Global warming and climate change are major factors in the spread of infectious disease. In South America, herbicides introduced into the pampas altered the ecology, leading to the creation of a new mouse that was the carrier of a deadly virus that produced Argentine hemorrhagic fever, a disease similar to Ebola.

In Africa, AIDS, Ebola, and other deadly new viral diseases emerged in areas characterized by banana plantations and other monocultures, the extraction of conflict metals, and uranium mining—all of which involve chemicals and toxins that can disrupt ecosystems and give rise to virulent new strains of viruses.

The worldwide decline of songbirds and frogs, to take another example, is leading to the catastrophic increase in mosquitoes, fleas, and other insects that spread viral and bacterial diseases. Global warming, the thinning of the protective ozone layer around the earth, and other environmental changes are key factors in the decline of biodiversity and rise of new diseases.

The origin and vector of COVID-19 in China remains uncertain. The toxins leading to the virulent new strain of coronavirus could be agricultural or connected with the manufacture of smartphones, plastic toys, or any number of other products. To prevent future epidemics from spreading from the soil to animal carriers and then to humans, it is imperative to transition to a natural and organic agriculture and food system.

Similarly, to prevent or treat corona and other viral diseases, it is important to maintain strong healthy blood, lymph, and other body fluids. These are the body's primary line of defense against contagious diseases and immune deficiency disorders. Along with known risk factors such as age, sex, and exposure to the microbe, they help determine whether any given individual will symptomatize and the mildness or severity of their infection.

The best way to build up natural immunity to contagious disease is to eat a strong, balanced, mineral rich diet, beginning with whole cereal grains, beans and bean products, miso soup; leafy green, round, and root vegetables; arame, wakame, nori, or other sea vegetables; homemade pickles or sauerkraut; fruit, seeds, nuts, mild grain-based sweeteners, spring or well water, and nonaromatic, non-stimulant beverages.

On the minus side of the dietary ledger, natural resistance to infection is compromised by eating animal-quality foods (with the exception of small amounts of white-meat fish), polished grains, cane sugar and other simple sugars, coffee and other stimulants, hot spices, alcohol, and foods grown with or containing chemicals, preservatives, and GMOs. Ultra-processed foods, which now make up about half the modern diet, should also be strictly avoided, including both the red-meat Big Mac and the vegan Impossible Burger.

We support the current worldwide mobilization to stem the coronavirus epidemic, including proper hygiene, quarantine, and development of a safe, effective vaccine. In our experience as dietary and way of life counselors dealing with patients with AIDS and other viral conditions over the years, we have found that Ume-Sho-Kuzu Drink to be highly beneficial for strengthening digestion, reducing inflammation, relieving infection, and helping the body discharge acidity. Miso soup, a traditional soup made with fermented soybean paste, wakame sea vegetables, and several seasonal vegetables, is also protective.

**Ume-Sho-Kuzu Drink**

1. Dissolve 1 heaping teaspoon of kuzu in 2-3 teaspoons of cold water.
2. Add 1 cup of cold water to the dissolved kuzu.
3. Bring to a boil over a medium flame, stirring constantly to avoid lumping, until the liquid becomes translucent. Reduce the flame to low.
4. Add the pulp of ½ to 1 umeboshi plum.

5. Add several drops to 1 teaspoon of shoyu/natural soy sauce and stir gently.
6. Simmer for 2-3 minutes. Drink hot.

*Ume* refers to umeboshi plum; *sho* to shoyu or natural soy sauce, and *kuzu* to kuzu (kudzu) root thickener. If kuzu is not available in the natural foods store or supermarket, use *kukicha* (bancha twig tea). If this is not available, just use water. The three ingredients in this traditional home remedy have been found to be beneficial to help relieve other potentially lethal viral conditions, as well as other serious disorders:

- Japanese medical researchers found that umeboshi contains a substance that can suppress the growth of the H1N1 virus that sparked the Swine Flu epidemic. When applied to affected cells, scientists reported, the growth of the virus was suppressed by nearly 90% after seven hours.[1]
- Kuzu, the creeping vine known as kudzu in the West, is a potent suppressor of HIV-1 cells, according to the journal *Retrovirology*. "Specifically, kudzu inhibits the initial attachment of the viral particle to the cell surface," the researchers reported. More than 90% inhibition was observed in the experiments. "Given kudzu's low cost, safety, oral bioavailability, tissue distribution, activity with ART [anti-retroviral therapy] and potent activity against HIV…it should be considered as a

promising supplement to current HIV therapeutic strategies."[2]

- The *British Medical Journal* reported early this year that miso and natto, fermented soy products originally from the Far East that are now produced in Europe, America, and other modern societies, were inversely associated with all causes of mortality, including respiratory diseases, in both sexes[3]

- Scientists at the National University of Singapore report that shoyu has antioxidant properties that are 10 times more potent than red wine, and 150 times more effective than vitamin C. It's the high concentration of brown pigment in shoyu that is thought to contribute to its strong antioxidant and anticancer properties. Shoyu aids in digestion and is rich in minerals.[4]

**Miso Soup**

2-inch piece of dried wakame sea vegetable
1 cup onions, sliced thinly
1 quart water
barley miso

Soak the wakame (about ¼-½-inch piece per person) for 5 minutes and cut into small pieces. Add the wakame to fresh, cold water and bring to a boil. Meanwhile, cut onions into small pieces. Add the vegetables to the boiling broth and boil all together for 3-5 minutes until the vegetables are soft and edible. Reduce flame to low. Dilute miso (½ to 1 level teaspoon per cup of broth) in a little water, add to soup, and simmer for 3-4 minutes on a low flame. Once the miso is added, don't boil the soup. Just let it simmer. Garnish with finely chopped scallions or parsley before serving.

- Be sure to simmer the soup for 3-4 minutes *after* miso paste is added to the broth. This is a very simple soup to make, but not letting the miso cook properly will reduce its effects
- For variety or a gluten-free miso, use brown rice miso or all soybean (hatcho). As a rule, misos for daily soup should be aged a minimum of 2 years. Misos may also be combined for a unique taste and flavor. Lighter red, yellow, and white miso make great dressings and sauces
- Vary the vegetables daily. Nice combinations include onions and tofu; onions and sweet autumn or winter squash; cabbage and carrots; and daikon and daikon greens
- Include leafy greens often in miso soup, including kale, collards, watercress, etc. Add them toward the end of cooking since they don't need to cook as long
- A small volume of shiitake mushrooms (soaked and finely chopped beforehand) may be added and cooked with the other vegetables from time to time
- For the most beneficial effect, miso soup should be cooked fresh each time and not stored overnight

Miso is well known for preventing cancer, heart disease, radiation sickness, and other chronic conditions and disorders. It is also effective to neutralize microbial afflictions:

- The *International Journal of Medical Sciences* reports that miso extracts are effective to "work as antivirals" against Hepatitis A Virus.[5]
- Several years ago, when the Ebola epidemic broke out in West Africa, we launched a web site with dietary advice for Ebola: www.ebolaanddiet.com. These guidelines were circulated widely, and we received a note of thanks from a major international airline with routes between West Africa and Europe and America that distributed the suggestions to their very alarmed staff and pilots.
- Dr. David W. Denning, Professor of Infectious Diseases in Global Health, University Hospital of South Manchester, UK, endorsed these recommendations: "Sensible and nutritious dietary advice and real behavior change is needed across the Western world. Red meat eating … contributes big time to water shortages and global warming as meat is an inefficient source of protein compared with fruit and vegetables … I suspect that even 2 days of macrobiotic food would be a great improvement on many people's diets … There is much your advocacy can offer the world."[6]

There are many healthful foods and safe, effective remedies that can promote natural immunity and, as part of an integrative medical campaign, help relieve the spreading coronavirus pandemic. Please seek immediate medical attention from your physician if you suspect that you have the coronavirus, and visit the websites listed in the Resource section at the back of the book.

The coronavirus crisis offers an opportunity for integrative medicine, combining the best allopathic and holistic approaches, to help resolve a global health emergency. If the focus remains only on suppressing the virus and eliminating its vectors, it may serve to intensify xenophobia, prejudice, and other polarizing tendencies. As a society, we must self-reflect and take responsibility for creating deadly epidemics through destructive agricultural, industrial, and environmental policies. By uniting together and reorienting in a more natural, organic, and sustainable direction, there is an excellent chance we can stem the contagion and make future outbreaks more unlikely.

When necessary, we will begin to limit the amount of people in the store. Please be prepared to wait outside or in your car if you arrive in a high volume moment. There are a few things you can do to help maintain social distancing in the stores: Whenever possible, please have only one family member do the shopping. Please give staff members (especially those who are stocking the shelves or produce section), extra space.

GUIDO'S FRESH MARKET, MARCH 2020

# MACROBIOTIC

*Dietary and Way of Life Suggestions*
*For persons living in a temperate climate*

**Daily Dietary Recommendations**

WHOLE CEREAL GRAINS. Between 40 and 50% by weight of every meal is recommended to include cooked, organically grown, whole cereal grains prepared in a variety of ways. Whole cereal grains include brown rice, barley, millet, whole wheat, rye, oats, corn, and buckwheat. Please note that a portion of this amount may consist of noodles or pasta, unyeasted whole grain breads, and other partially processed whole cereal grains.

SOUPS. 1-2 cups or bowls (about 5-10%) of your daily food intake may include soup made with vegetables, sea vegetables (wakame or kombu) grains, or beans. Seasonings are usually miso or shoyu (organic soy sauce.) The flavor should not be too salty.

VEGETABLES. About 25-30% of daily intake may include local and organically grown vegetables. Preferably, the majority is cooked in various styles (e.g. sautéed with a small amount of vegetable oil, steamed, boiled, and sometimes as raw salad or naturally fermented or pickled vegetables.

Vegetables for daily use include green cabbage, kale, broccoli, cauliflower, collards, pumpkin, watercress, Chinese cabbage, bok choy, dandelion, mustard greens, daikon greens, scallion, onion, daikon, turnip, various fall and summer squashes, burdock, carrot, varieties.

Avoid or limit the intake of potato (including sweet potato and yam), tomato, eggplant, pepper, spinach, asparagus, beet, zucchini, and avocado. Mayonnaise and other oily, fatty, or artificial dressings are best avoided.

BEANS AND SEA VEGETABLES. ¼ to ½ cup (about 5-10%) of the daily diet may include cooked beans and sea vegetables. Beans for regular use include azuki, chickpea, lentil, and black soybean, as well as kidney, navy, black bean, white beans, pinto, non-GMO soybean, and others. Bean products such as tofu, tempeh, and natto can also be used. Sea vegetables such as wakame, nori, kombu, hiziki, arame, dulse, agar, and others may be prepared in a variety of ways. They can be cooked with beans or vegetables, used in soups, or served separately as side dishes or salads, moderately flavored with brown rice vinegar, sea salt, shoyu, ume plum, and other natural seasonings.

OCCASIONAL FOODS. Animal quality food is optional. If needed or desired, 1-3 times a week, approximately 10% of the daily consumption of food can include fresh wild caught flaky white meat fish. Non-farm raised salmon and sea scallops can be included several times per month if your condition permits.

Fruit or fruit desserts, including fresh, dried, and cooked fruits, may also be served three or four times per week on average. Local and organically grown fruits are preferred. If you live in a temperate climate, avoid tropical and semi-tropical fruit and eat, instead, temperate climate fruits such as apples, pears, plums, peaches, nectarines, apricots, berries, and melons. Local organic fruit juice may also be consumed if your condition permits.

Lightly roasted nuts and seeds such as pumpkin, sesame, and sunflower may be enjoyed as snacks, together with peanuts, walnuts, almonds, and pecans.

Rice syrup, barley malt, amasake, and mirin may be used as sweeteners, together with occasional maple syrup. Brown rice vinegar, lemon, or umeboshi vinegar may be used for a sour taste.

BEVERAGES. Recommended daily beverages include bancha (kukicha) twig tea, stem tea, roasted brown rice and barley tea, and occasional dandelion and corn silk tea. Any traditional tea that does not have an aromatic fragrance or a stimulating effect can be used. You may also drink a comfortable amount of water (preferably spring or well water of good quality) but not iced.

FOODS TO REDUCE OR AVOID. Meat, animal fat, eggs, poultry, dairy products (including butter, yogurt, ice cream, milk, and cheese), fatty fish and seafood, refined sugars, chocolate, molasses, honey, other simple sugars like stevia, agave, evaporated cane juice, etc., and foods treated with them.

Tropical or semi-tropical fruits and fruit juices, including banana and pineapple, soda, artificial drinks and beverages, coffee, colored tea, and all aromatic stimulating teas such as mint or peppermint.

All artificially colored, preserved, sprayed, or chemically treated foods, including foods with GMO ingredients. All refined and polished grains, flours, and their derivatives. Mass-produced industrialized food including canned, frozen, and irradiated foods.

Hot spices, any aromatic stimulating food or food accessory, artificial vinegar, and strong alcoholic beverages, especially those produced from sugar or mixed with sugared beverages.

ADDITIONAL SUGGESTIONS

Cooking oil should be vegetable quality only, with natural cold pressed olive and sesame as preferred varieties.

Salt should be naturally processed sea salt. Traditional, non-chemical shoyu or tamari soy sauce and miso may be used as seasonings.

Recommended condiments include:

— Gomashio (sesame salt made from approx. 20 parts roasted sesame seeds to one part sea salt)
— Sea vegetable powder or flakes, including green

nori, dulse, kelp, wakame and others, as well as combinations or blends
— Sesame seed wakame powder
— Umeboshi plum
— Tekka
— Roasted seeds such as sunflower or pumpkin

Pickled vegetables made without sugar or strong spice, including non-pasteurized organic sauerkraut, pickled Chinese cabbage, and others may be eaten on a daily basis.

You may have meals regularly, 2-3 times per day, as much as you want, provided the proportion is correct and the chewing is thorough. Avoid eating for approximately 3 hours before sleeping.

THE IMPORTANCE OF COOKING. Proper cooking is very important for health. Everyone should learn to cook either by attending classes or under the guidance of an experienced macrobiotic cook. The recipes included in macrobiotic cookbooks may also be used in planning meals.

SPECIAL ADVICE
The guidelines present above are general suggestions. These suggestions may require modification depending on your individual condition. Of course, any serious condition should be closely monitored by the appropriate medical, nutritional, and health professional.

Together with beginning to change your diet, we invite you to attend regular seminars, cooking classes, and study programs and to meet with a qualified macrobiotic counselor or educator.

Way of Life Suggestions

- Live each day happily without being preoccupied with your health; try to keep mentally and physically active.
- View everything and everyone you meet with gratitude, particularly offering thanks before and after each meal.
- Chew your food very well, at least 50 times per mouthful, or until it becomes liquid.
- It is best to retire before midnight and get up early every morning.
- It is best to avoid wearing synthetic or woolen clothing directly on the skin. As much as possible, wear cotton, especially for undergarments. Avoid excessive metallic accessories on the fingers, wrists, or neck. Keep such ornaments simple and graceful.
- Take a ½ hour walk each day. When safe and appropriate, walk barefoot on grass, beach, or soil. Keep your home in good order, from the kitchen, bathroom, bedroom, and living quarters, to every corner of the house.
- Initiate and maintain an active correspondence, extending your best wishes to parents, children, brothers and sisters, teachers, and friends.

- Avoid taking long hot showers or baths unless you have been consuming too much salt or animal food.
- To increase circulation, scrub your entire body with a hot, damp towel every morning. If that is not possible, at least scrub your hands, feet, fingers and toes.
- Avoid chemically perfumed cosmetics. For care of the teeth, brush with natural, fluoride-free preparations.
- If your condition permits, exercise regularly as part of daily life, including activities like walking, scrubbing floors, cleaning windows, washing clothes and working in the garden. You may also participate in exercise programs such as yoga, martial arts, dance, or sports.
- Avoid using electric cooking devices (stoves, ovens, ranges) or microwave ovens. Convert to gas cooking at the earliest opportunity.
- It is best to minimize the use of color television, computer monitors, cellphones, tablets, smartphones, and other mobile devices.
- Include large green plants in your house to freshen and enrich the oxygen content of the air in your home. Open windows frequently to permit air to circulate freely.
- Sing a happy song every day.

What is the most fundamental way to restore natural immunity? Our blood, including the immune cells, is made from what we eat. By changing our food, we change the plasma, or liquid portion of the blood, and also the red blood cells and lymphocytes, including T-cells and B-cells.

Michio Kushi

# SPECIAL REMEDIES

## LOTUS ROOT TEA

Lotus root tea is a standard macrobiotic remedy for eliminating mucus in the respiratory system and to ease coughing. This tea is most effective when prepared from fresh lotus root. However, if fresh lotus is not available, you may use dried lotus root or lotus root powder.

### With fresh lotus root:

Wash the root and grate one-half cup. Place the pulp in a piece of cheesecloth and squeeze the juice into a bowl or cup. You may also place the gratings in your palm and squeeze the juice with your fingers. Place the juice in a saucepan with an equal amount of water. Add a pinch of sea salt or a few drops of shoyu/soy sauce. Bring to a boil, and let simmer gently on a low flame for 2-3 minutes. Drink this tea, which should be thick and creamy, while hot. You may also add a few drops of grated ginger juice toward the end if your condition permits to warm the body and loosen stagnation.

### With dried lotus root:

Place one-third ounce (about 1/4 cup) of dried lotus root in one cup of water. Let it sit for a few minutes until soft, then chop finely. Return the finely chopped lotus root to the soaking water. Add a pinch of sea salt or a few drops of shoyu/soy sauce. Bring to a boil and simmer gently for approximately 15 minutes. Strain the liquid and drink while hot. You may also add a few drops of grated ginger juice at the end if your condition permits.

### With lotus root powder:
Use one teaspoon of lotus powder per person and per serving. Add one cup of cold water per teaspoon of powder and stir to dissolve. Add a pinch of sea salt or a few drops of shoyu/soy sauce. You may also add a couple of drops of grated ginger juice if your condition permits. Heat on a low flame but don't bring to a boil. Turn off the heat when the liquid begins to simmer. Drink hot.

### DAIKON DRINK
This variation of grated daikon tea helps lower fever by inducing sweat. It can also bring relief from poisoning caused by meat, fish, or shellfish.

Grate about three tablespoons of fresh daikon. Mix the daikon with one-quarter teaspoon grated ginger and a few drops of shoyu/soy sauce. Pour one cup of hot bancha twig or stem tea over the mixed ingredients. Drink as much of the tea as possible while hot. After drinking this tea, go to bed and wrap yourself in a blanket to induce perspiration. Since this tea is very strong, do not take more than twice a day for one or two days. To reduce fever in children, it is best to give apple juice, grated apple, or a kuzu drink with rice syrup (dissolve one teaspoon of kuzu in two teaspoons of cold water. Add one teaspoon of rice syrup. Bring to a gentle boil over a medium flame while stirring and turn off the flame as soon as the drink has thickened and become translucent.

## TOFU PLASTER

Traditionally known to help with concussions, hemorrhoid, fever, and burns, in many cases, more effectively than ice.

Squeeze out the liquid from a block of tofu and mash tofu in a suribachi, or traditional clay grinding bowl. Add 2-3 tbsp. unbleached white flour and 1 tsp. grated ginger (optional.) Mix well. Apply the mixture directly to the skin and cover with a towel. You may want to secure it with a bandage, or tie with a cotton strip. Change the plaster when it becomes hot.

## UME SHO KUZU

Medical researchers in Japan have found that umeboshi plums, a traditional salted, aged, pickled plum and a staple in the macrobiotic way of eating, contain a substance that can suppress the growth of the H1N1 virus that led to the Swine Flu epidemic several years ago. When applied to affected cells, researchers reported, the growth of the virus was suppressed by near 90 percent after seven hours. –"Umeboshi have H1N1 Suppressant," *Japan Times*, June 3, 2010

Umeboshi help the body neutralize strong acids. When used in combination with kuzu root, a deep root with strengthening and fortifying properties, umeboshi helps neutralize toxins, restore energy, and cancel the digestive disorders that accompany virus infection. (For further information, see *How the Umeboshi Works*, by Edward Esko, IMI Press, 2019.)

Dissolve one heaping teaspoon (for children) and one heaping tablespoon (for adults) of kuzu in two to three tablespoons of cold water. Add one cup of water to the dissolved kuzu. Heat over a medium flame. Stir to prevent lumping. When the liquid approaches a boil, it will become translucent and thicken. At that point reduce the heat to low. Add the pulp of one-half to one umeboshi plum. Add several drops to one teaspoon of shoyu/soy sauce and stir gently. Simmer for two to three minutes, pour into a mug or bowl, and drink hot.

# SUMMARY
# RECOMMENDATIONS

- Boil or pressure-cook short grain brown rice daily, preferably on a gas stove, with a small pinch of sea salt
- Make soft rice kayu (porridge) for breakfast. Eat with condiments such as umeboshi plum and nori
- Include foods such as small white or yellow beans, root vegetables like burdock, lotus, and carrot, hiziki sea vegetable, hard autumn fruits like apple and pear, and beverages such as roasted brown rice tea
- Balance with foods such as raw scallion and chive (as garnish), barley, dandelion and other leafy greens, brown rice vinegar, and sour apple and lemon
- Include naturally fermented foods to strengthen the microbiome and immune system on a daily basis, for example miso soup, sauerkraut, natto, tempeh, pickles, etc.
- Eat wakame, nori, dulse, arame, and other sea vegetables daily in soup, side dishes, and as dried condiments

- Cook every day and keep your meals as fresh as possible
- Chew well and don't eat before bed
- Minimize exposure to electronic or wireless devices, including smartphones and laptops

# Guidelines for Shopping and Food Storage

The staple foods in a macrobiotic diet are perfect for storing at room temperature in a clean dry pantry, cellar, or spare room. Make sure they are properly packaged and sealed. The dry goods listed below can be purchased in bulk and put aside for use. It is recommended that during a pandemic or other emergency, individuals and families purchase at least a six-week supply of basic staples. The guidelines below represent only a sample of the healthful naturally storable foods that are recommended for individuals and families. Certified organic products are preferred.

**GRAINS**
Brown rice (short-, medium-, long-grain)
Barley (both un-hulled and lightly pearled)
Millet
Oats
Quinoa
Wheat, rye, spelt
Dried and popping corn

Oatmeal, corn meal, whole grits, and other whole grain breakfast cereals

Whole grain noodles and pasta, including udon, soba, somen, and others

Whole organic noodles made from beans or vegetables.

Organic sourdough bread (can be frozen for future use)

## BEANS
Azuki

Chickpea

Lentil

Kidney

Other dried or canned (no-salt, BPH-free) beans

Items such as organic tofu, tempeh, and natto are recommended, but need to be bought fresh and locally as they are perishable

## SEASONING
Miso

Shoyu (soy sauce)

Brown rice vinegar

Sea salt

Umeboshi plum, paste, vinegar

## DRIED VEGETABLES
Shiitake mushroom

Dried daikon radish

Dried burdock root

Kuzu root powder

## SEA VEGETABLES
Wakame
Nori
Dulse
Kombu
Arame
Kelp and digitata (Atlantic kombu)
Alaria (Atlantic wakame)
Bladderwrack

## CONDIMENTS
Maine Coast dulse and vegetable powders
Gomashio (sesame salt)
Edenshake (furikake)
Homemade sea vegetable and sesame seed condiments
Umeboshi plum and paste
Tekka, dried shiso, and other specialty condiments

## BEVERAGE
Kukicha twig tea (bancha)
Roasted barley tea
Organic green tea
Dandelion tea
Burdock root tea
Corn silk tea

## PICKLES
Sauerkraut
Kimchee (mild)
Traditional non-spicy, non-sweetened vegetable pickles

## SWEETENERS
Apple cider
Dried apple, apricot, raisin, and other local fruit
Amasake
Brown rice syrup
Maple syrup

## COOKING OIL
Olive, sesame, sunflower, and other naturally cold-pressed vegetable oils

## PRODUCE
Fresh vegetables, fruits, seeds and nuts, and other perishable items can be purchased as needed from local organic, conventional, and natural food markets, as well as directly from farmers and farmer's markets. Specialty rations, such as canned or frozen vegetables and other foods, may also be necessary to supplement one's diet during a pandemic or other emergency.

## MAIL ORDER SUPPLIERS
Many of the above high-quality organic staples are available online, both in small quantities or in bulk from:

### Eden Foods
Clinton, MI
Edenfoods.com

### Natural Import Company
Asheville, NC
Naturalimport.com

**Goldmine Natural Foods**
San Diego, CA
Goldminenaturalfoods.com

**Maine Seaweed**
Steuben, ME
TheSeaweedMan.com

**Maine Coast Sea Vegetables**
Hancock, ME
SeaVeg.com

**South River Miso**
Conway, MA
SouthRiverMiso.com

# APPENDIX

## *COOKING BROWN RICE*

Brown rice is ideal for strengthening the lungs and large intestine. In oriental medicine, brown rice was thought to share the energetic characteristic, known as condensed or gathering "metal" energy, of the lung and large intestine. Brown rice is easy to digest and free of gluten. The undigested fiber in whole rice serves as a prebiotic nutrient. It ferments in the colon and enhances the colonies of beneficial bacteria that strengthen natural immunity. Moreover, when we cook brown rice (and other whole grains), we are utilizing and managing the basic elements that make life possible.

The first element is the rice (or other whole grain) itself. For a temperate climate, we suggest using short grain organic brown rice on a regular basis. Other whole grain varieties, such as medium grain and basmati, can be used for variety or to adapt to climatic and seasonal variation. Pure clean water is the second element. Water quality has become a huge headache in the modern world. Municipal water is chemically treated and often fluoridated and is not suitable for daily use. As a result, we recommend using natural spring or well water. Filtered, but not distilled, water can also be used.

Salt is the next element. Try to locate high quality natural sea salt. Grey salt is not recommended as it has too high a content of magnesium. After experimenting with a variety of natural sea salts, we selected *Si Salt,* processed from the clean Pacific waters off Baja, California as suitable for daily use. Other salts can also be used. Keep in mind that when adding salt to your brown rice, only a pinch is needed.

The fourth element is fire. As with water, the quality of fire is problematic today. Cooking with fire has been replaced with artificial electric ranges and microwave ovens, both of which impart unnatural and potentially harmful radiation and both of which take away the delicate control necessary for healthful cooking. For this reason we recommend cooking over a gas flame. (Note that most gourmet chefs prefer to cook on a gas range.)

### Basic Brown Rice (Tight-Lid Boiling Method)

1. Wash one cup of organic brown rice by covering with water, rinsing, and draining the water. Repeat three times.
2. Place in a pot with a tight-fitting lid. Add a small pinch of sea salt (optional) and 1 ½ - 2 cups of spring water.
3. Cover and bring to a boil on a medium high flame. When the rice comes to an active boil, reduce the flame to low and cook for 50-60 minutes.
4. Turn off the flame and let the rice sit for several minutes.

5. Remove from the pot with a wooden spoon and place in a serving bowl.

Brown rice may also be cooked in a pressure cooker from time to time. Bring 1 cup of washed grain to a boil in 1 ½ cups wa¬ter and when pressure is up, place a flame de¬flector under the pot. Lower the flame and cook for 50 minutes. Brown rice and other whole grains can also be soaked prior to cooking, any¬where from one to several hours or even overnight depending upon one's condition and needs.

# Resources

**Berkshire Holistic Associates (BHA)** is a division of the non-profit Planetary Health, Inc, a Berkshire-based 501(c)(3) educational organization. Founded by Edward Esko, Alex Jack, and Bettina Zumdick, BHA is dedicated to providing quality and affordable education on the benefits of a plant-based diet. BHA also supports adoption of complementary healthcare approaches such as acupuncture, massage, Asian bodywork, and yoga, and serves as a referral for these services in Berkshire County. BerkshireHolistic.com.

**Planetary Health/Amberwaves**, PO Box 487, Becket MA 01223, 413-623-0012, email: shenwa@bcn.net, www.macrobioticsummerconference.com. A grassroots network devoted to preserving amber waves of grain and keeping America and the planet beautiful through macrobiotic education and research. PH is a 501(c)(3) non-profit organization. It publishes books and articles by macrobiotic authors, educators, and Planetary Health co-founders, Alex Jack and Edward Esko, and sponsors the annual Macrobiotic Summer Conference and research on the macrobiotic way of life.

**International Macrobiotic Institute.** Macrobiotic education with Edward Esko and associates, featuring the

Macrobiotic Online Course, an online certificate course with three levels of study. Based in Massachusetts, with affiliates in New York, Dubai, Abu Dhabi, Barcelona, Vietnam, Australia, and Kuala Lumpur. Visit: InternationalMacrobioticInstitute.com.

**Macrobiotics Today/George Ohsawa Macrobiotic Foundation (GOMF)**, 1277 Marian Ave., Chico CA 95928, 800-232-2372, OhsawaMacrobiotics.com. A macrobiotic publisher and educational center on the West Coast.

**The Barnard Medical Center** combines medical care with the latest advances in prevention and nutrition to create a health care plan designed for each client. If you need to treat and reverse diabetes, heart disease, high blood pressure, or other chronic conditions, the Barnard Medical Center will help you revolutionize your health. Visit: www. BarnardMedicalCenter.com.

**The Culinary Medicine School** is a center for healing, transformation, and awareness in Lee, Mass. Founded and directed by Bettina Zumdick the CMS offers studies and workshops in culinary medicine, self-care, and private chef services. CulinaryMedicineSchool.com or contact Bettina at 413-429-5610 for information.

**Sommer White, M.D.** Vitality Medical Center, 125 Belle Forest Circle, Suite 100, Nashville, TN 37221. Tel: 615-891-7500, www.sommerwhitemd.com. Holistic, macrobiotic, and integrative medicine and nutrition presented by a Kushi Institute graduate.

**Macrobiotics America**. Online education with David and Cindy Briscoe. Certificate courses, special workshops, products, and recipes. Located in Oroville, CA. Visit. www. MacroAmerica.com.

**Christina Cooks.** Cooking classes, books, products, travel, and info from a leading macrobiotic and vegan teacher, author, and chef. Located in Philadelphia, PA. Visit: ChristinaCooks.com.

**Strengthening Health Institute.** Online and in-person education with Denny and Susan Waxman. Certificate courses, special workshops, recipes, blog and more. Located in Philadelphia, PA. Visit: shimacrobiotics.org.

**MacroVegan.** Online and in-person workshops with Bill Tara and Marlene Watson-Tara. Courses, workshops, cooking classes, videos, books, and counseling with leading macrobiotic vegan authors and teachers. Located near London, England. Visit: MacroVegan.org.

# RECOMMENDED READING

Esko, Edward. *Alzheimer's: The Macrobiotic Approach*, IMI Press, Lenox, Mass., 2019.

Esko, Edward. *How the Umeboshi Works*, IMI Press, Lenox, Mass., 2019.

Esko, Edward. *Macrobiotic Nutrition: A Guide to Sustainable Plant-based Eating,* IMI Press, Lenox, Mass., 2018.

Esko, Edward. With Alex Jack and Bettina Zumdick. *Crohn's and Colitis: A Whole Food Plant Based Approach.* Berkshire Holistic Associates, Becket, Mass., 2019.

Esko, Edward. With Alex Jack and Bettina Zumdick. *Diabetes: A Whole Food Plant Based Approach.* Berkshire Holistic Associates, Becket, Mass., 2019.

Jack, Alex and Sachi Kato, *The One Peaceful World Cookbook.* BenBella Books, Dallas, Texas, 2017.

Kushi, Aveline and Wendy Esko. *The Changing Seasons Macrobiotic Cookbook.* Avery Trade, Garden City Park, New York, 2003.

Kushi, Aveline and Alex Jack, *Aveline Kushi's Complete Guide to Macrobiotic Cooking.* Time-Warner, New York, New York, 1985.

Kushi, Michio and Marc Van Cauwenberghe, M.D. *Macrobiotic Home Remedies: Your Guide to Traditional Healing Techniques.* Square One Publishers, Garden City Park, New York, 2015.

Kushi, Michio and Martha Cottrell, M.D. *AIDS, Macrobiotics, and Natural Immunity.* Japan Publications, Tokyo and New York, 1991.

Kushi, Michio and Alex Jack. *The Book of Macrobiotics: The Universal Way of Health and Happiness.* Square One Publishers, Garden City Park, New York, 2012.

Kushi, Michio. *The Do-In Way: Gentle Exercises to Liberate the Body, Mind, and Spirit.* Square One Publishers, Garden City Park, New York, 2009.

Kushi, Michio. *Your Body Never Lies: The Complete Book of Oriental Diagnosis.* Square One Publishers, Garden City Park, New York, 2010.

Muramoto, Noburo. *Natural Immunity: Insights on Diet and AIDS.* George Ohsawa Macrobiotic Foundation, Oroville, California, 1988.

Pirello, Christina. *Back to the Cutting Board*. BenBella Books, Dallas, Texas, 2018.

Tara. Bill. *How to Eat Right and Save the Planet*. Square One Publishers, Garden City Park, New York, 2020.

Waxman, Denny and Susan Waxman. *The Ultimate Guide to Eating for Longevity*. Pegasus Books, New York, London, 2019.

Zumdick, Bettina. *Authentic Foods*. Amberwaves Press, 2012.

# Also From Berkshire Holistic Associates

ISBN: 9798615718380

ISBN: 9781713199076

ISBN: 9781706408185

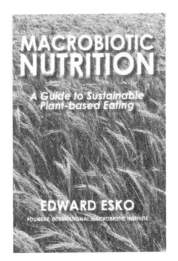

ISBN: 978-1721970070

# ENDNOTES

1   "Umeboshi Have H1N1 Suppressant," *Japan Times*, June 3, 2010.

2   S. Mediouni et al. "Potent suppression of HIV-1 cell attachment by Kudzu root extract," *Retrovirology* 2018:15:64.

3   R. Katagiri et al., "Association of soy and fermented soy product intake with total and cause specific mortality: prospective cohort study," *British Medical Journal* Jan 29, 2020:368m34.

4   Wang, Huansong et al., "The identification of antioxidants in dark soy sauce," *Free radical research*, 2007:41. 479-88.

5   Nan New Win et al., "Inhibitory effect of Japanese rice-koji miso extracts on hepatitis A virus replication in association with the elevation of glucose-regulated protein 78 expression," *International Journal of Medical Sciences*, July 30, 2018.

6   Personal email communication to Alex Jack from David W. Denning, Autumn 2013.

Printed in Great Britain
by Amazon